1 —

Amazing Websites & Apps
Easy Do-It-Yourself
David K. Ewen, M.Ed.

— 1

Amazing Websites & Apps

Easy Do-It-Yourself

By:

David K. Ewen, M.Ed.

ISBN-13: 978-1508557982
ISBN-10: 1508557985

Amazing Websites & Apps
Easy Do-It-Yourself
David K. Ewen, M.Ed.

Contents

Amazing Websites & Apps
Easy Do-It-Yourself

By

David K. Ewen, M.Ed.

Amazing Websites & Apps
Easy Do-It-Yourself
David K. Ewen, M.Ed.

This book is the culmination of years experience in website and mobile app development that eventually evolved into part of a three hour lecture conference to train individuals on the topic. This subject is part of the "Professor Lecture Series" that is held in the seven states of New York and New England. The series began in June 2004 in Massachusetts and has spread to New York and all of New England.

In addition to Websites and mobile apps development, other courses in computer technology are included as part of the "Professor Lecture Series". they include among others, Excel, PowerPoint, Blogging, Windows 8, and QuickBooks. Some other technical topics include publishing, broadcasting, recording, and other digital multimedia technologies.

Ten years before the "Professor Lecture Series" was launched, Ewen Prime Company was launched as a book publishing house. That was in 1994. After that, broadcasting on WORC 1310 AM & WGFP 940 AM began what Would the beginning of a broadcasting career and the start of the EPN network and EPN NEWS. With a variety of media, technology, and communications experience, the author David K. Ewen, M.Ed. shares his experience through Lectures that are face-to-face an online as well as a variety of content in print, Recorded, and on video. More can be found at www.ForestAcademy.org

5 —

Amazing Websites & Apps
Easy Do-It-Yourself
David K. Ewen, M.Ed.

— 5

Create Websites
Fast and Easy
to Save Money

Amazing Websites & Apps
Easy Do-It-Yourself
David K. Ewen, M.Ed.

The goal of this course is to teach students how to create amazing websites and mobile apps without special technical knowledge. Many tools learned in this course can be applied to other knowledge areas beyond websites and mobile apps. This course will provide a good solid understanding of the tools that are available on the internet. The tools discussed in this course are free and widely available. With so many free tools available, it is unlikely one person knows all of them. You'll have a chance to explore many of them in this course.

The kind of website development discussed in this course is template driven. That means the websites that you will design is made in a fill-in-the-blank sort of way with a few clicks and drags of the mouse to position elements of an amazing website.   Behind the scenes, the websites being developed are being coded in a language called HTML5. That means it works both on a regular computer and mobile device.   So you are actually developing the mobile app at the same time you are developing the website.

Amazing Websites & Apps
8 —   Easy Do-It-Yourself   — 8
David K. Ewen, M.Ed.

The mobile apps that students will learn to create use very simple tools. There are 2 kinds of mobile apps available. One kind is the one that needs to be downloaded from a store like Google Play or iTunes. Those kinds of apps require permissions and update information on your phone and take ups storage space. The 2nd kind of mobile app is a web link that is pinned to the home screen of your mobile device. This type of app is compatible with any mobile device. It doesn't matter if the device is an Android or iPhone product. This is the kind of mobile app students will learn to create in this course.

9 —

Amazing Websites & Apps
Easy Do-It-Yourself
David K. Ewen, M.Ed.

— 9

Students don't need to learn about complicated coding techniques or download large software tools that require complex knowledge. If they know who to navigate a website and use mobile apps, then this course Is the right one for them.

It's one thing to create a website and mobile app. It's another thing to let people know about it. This course includes the simple steps to distribute the website and mobile apps to users. So you'll create a website and mobile app that you will distribute.

Amazing Websites & Apps
Easy Do-It-Yourself
David K. Ewen, M.Ed.

Websites are intended to

Brand awareness
Share information
Distribute content
Build businesses
Market & sell
Make money

The website you create will do all of that.

Amazing Websites & Apps
Easy Do-It-Yourself
David K. Ewen, M.Ed.

You'll learn advanced topics in an easy-to-understand way such as

URL, SERP, SEO, SMO, Meta Tags, SDK, CPC, & CPA
Content that is Public Domain and Royalty Free
Creative Commons License
Search Engine Optimization Tools
Social Media Marketing Techniques
Resources for Software Development Kits

You'll know the business of website & mobile app development

12 —

Amazing Websites & Apps
Easy Do-It-Yourself
David K. Ewen, M.Ed.

— **12**

Domain Name

13 —

Amazing Websites & Apps
Easy Do-It-Yourself
David K. Ewen, M.Ed.

— 13

The website development taught in this class results in a link that is longer than a domain name. A domain name is in the form of www._(something)_.com or another suffix, such as *.org, or *.net. There are others, but these are the most common.

The websites this course refers to will need a domain name from a company like "GoDaddy" (www.GoDaddy.com) or "Register" (www.Register.com) that requires an annual fee to remain active. These domain names will be used to point to the web link that will represent the website.

An example of our discussion is the domain name **www._sample_.com** will point to a much longer web link such as

 (name you pick).webs.com   or   __(your ID)_.wix.com/_(name you pick_)

The tool to create he website is free. The domain name is at the cost of a low annual fee.

14 —

Amazing Websites & Apps
Easy Do-It-Yourself
David K. Ewen, M.Ed.

— **14**

Getting a domain name doesn't need to be a first step. In fact, depending on how the website is used, you may not need one at all.   If you find you need a website that begins with WWW and ends in something like *.com, *.net, or *.org, then at some point, you will need to go to a site that sells domain names that you can register and forward to the web URL that you are creating.

A URL is called Universal Resource Locater.   It is a fancy name for a longer website link that is not a domain name.   Some examples are:

(name you pick).webs.com   or   **__(your ID)_.wix.com/_(name you pick_)**

To get a domain name, you can create an ID & Password at either of the following sites.

www.GoDaddy.com or **www.Register.com**   Shop around for the best prices.

15 —

Amazing Websites & Apps
Easy Do-It-Yourself
David K. Ewen, M.Ed.

— 15

Pictures

16 —

Amazing Websites & Apps
Easy Do-It-Yourself
David K. Ewen, M.Ed.

— 16

The first thing people think about when creating a website is to think of what kind of a logo would look good to brand the website and what it represents.

The logo involves words and pictures. Most logos are as simple as that.

17 — Amazing Websites & Apps
Easy Do-It-Yourself
David K. Ewen, M.Ed.

— **17**

You have to be careful about the pictures you use for your logo. If you download them from the internet, you may not be allowed to use it on public site such as your website. It is important to know how to recognize what you can use.

18 —

Amazing Websites & Apps
Easy Do-It-Yourself
David K. Ewen, M.Ed.

— **18**

Content found on the web come in the following categories:

Copyright protection
Royalty Free with license costs
Public Domain
Creative Commons

19 —

Amazing Websites & Apps
Easy Do-It-Yourself
David K. Ewen, M.Ed.

— **19**

Content under copyright protection are not authorized to be used without specific permission from the owner. In general it is best not to use content that is under copyright protection. If you don't know if it is under copyright protection, then assume it is.

20 —

Amazing Websites & Apps
Easy Do-It-Yourself
David K. Ewen, M.Ed.

— **20**

The copyright symbol is recognized by the C with a circle around it. Avoid using content that has copyright protection.

21 —

Amazing Websites & Apps
Easy Do-It-Yourself
David K. Ewen, M.Ed.

— 21

Many people think that Royalty Free content is FREE. It is not. It requires a one time licensing fee up front. The use of the content is free after that because it is Royalty Free. A royalty is a fee paid every time the content is used. Content that is Royalty Free does not have costs beyond the initial licensing fee for use.

Amazing Websites & Apps
22 —   Easy Do-It-Yourself   — 22
David K. Ewen, M.Ed.

Public domain content is royalty free and license free. This is content that is free to use. You may see symbols that indicate content is public domain, for example:

23 —

Amazing Websites & Apps
Easy Do-It-Yourself
David K. Ewen, M.Ed.

— **23**

Similar to content that is public domain, is content that is under the Creative Commons license. It is either public domain or under copyright protection, but authorized to be used as public domain content. There may be some restrictions, but usually it is treated as public domain.

When looking for pictures to use for your logo or for your website, consider using content under the creative commons license. You'll recognize content under this license with this symbol:

25 —

Amazing Websites & Apps
Easy Do-It-Yourself
David K. Ewen, M.Ed.

— **25**

Wikimedia Commons is a database of freely usable media files to which anyone can contribute. It is a create resource that includes images, sounds, and videos. It is located at: **http://commons.wikimedia.org**. To get pictures, you can click on IMAGES. You can also search for content by searching in the tool bar.

Amazing Websites & Apps
26 —   Easy Do-It-Yourself   — 26
David K. Ewen, M.Ed.

To find content that is under the Creative Commons license, go to:

http://commons.wikimedia.org

is a database of freely usable media files to which anyone can contribute.

27 —

Amazing Websites & Apps
Easy Do-It-Yourself
David K. Ewen, M.Ed.

— **27**

You can create your logo using a picture that is under the creative commons license:

http://commons.wikimedia.org

Add designer text, and you'll have a great logo.

28 —

Amazing Websites & Apps
Easy Do-It-Yourself
David K. Ewen, M.Ed.

— 28

Text Design

29 —

Amazing Websites & Apps
Easy Do-It-Yourself
David K. Ewen, M.Ed.

— **29**

A logo is attractive when the logo has a stylish look to it with fancy looking text. You can create text as a JPG file that can be combined with an image or picture.

30 —

Amazing Websites & Apps
Easy Do-It-Yourself
David K. Ewen, M.Ed.

— **30**

Cool Text is a FREE graphics generator for web pages and anywhere else you need an impressive logo without a lot of design work.   Go to:

http://cooltext.com

Also try: http://www.flamingtext.com

31 —

Amazing Websites & Apps
Easy Do-It-Yourself
David K. Ewen, M.Ed.

— **31**

Remember, for pictures, you will get pictures that are under the Creative Commons license. This way you won't be at risk of using content that is under copyright protection. Go to:

http://commons.wikimedia.org

Pictures:

http://commons.wikimedia.org

Text:

http://cooltext.com   &
http://www.flamingtext.com

33 —

Amazing Websites & Apps
Easy Do-It-Yourself
David K. Ewen, M.Ed.

— **33**

Image Editing

34 —

Amazing Websites & Apps
Easy Do-It-Yourself
David K. Ewen, M.Ed.

— **34**

Logos and banners need to be cropped and resized.   A simple way to do that is to use an online editor. It's easy to upload your images and edit them in your browser.   The online photo editor allows you to edit, crop, rotate and resize images. It's FREE to do.

35 —

Amazing Websites & Apps
Easy Do-It-Yourself
David K. Ewen, M.Ed.

— **35**

Here are some online image editors

http://**LunaPic.com** & http://**Blibs.com**
(http://www166.LunaPic.com/editor)

https://**pixlr.com**

http://www.PicMonkey.com

Amazing Websites & Apps
36 —   Easy Do-It-Yourself   — **36**
David K. Ewen, M.Ed.

You can download pictures to edit that are under the creative common license.

Go to:

http://commons.wikimedia.org

37 —

Amazing Websites & Apps
Easy Do-It-Yourself
David K. Ewen, M.Ed.

— **37**

Pictures
From PPT

Amazing Websites & Apps
38 —   Easy Do-It-Yourself   — 38
David K. Ewen, M.Ed.

When creating a logo or banner that uses text graphics and images, they will need to be combined together to make one final image.   PowerPoint is used to do that. The image and graphical text is imported into PowerPoint.   You can add other text features using Word Art from PowerPoint.

39 —

Amazing Websites & Apps
Easy Do-It-Yourself
David K. Ewen, M.Ed.

— **39**

Pictures:

http://commons.wikimedia.org

Text:

http://cooltext.com &
http://www.flamingtext.com

Here are some online image editors to be used on the pictures and graphical text before they are imported to PowerPoint.

http://**LunaPic.com** & http://**Blibs.com**
 (http://www166.LunaPic.com/editor)

https://**pixlr.com**

http://www.PicMonkey.com

41 —

Amazing Websites & Apps
Easy Do-It-Yourself
David K. Ewen, M.Ed.

— **41**

Within PowerPoint, a single slide is used to be the foundation that holds the picture and graphical text. The DESIGN tab is used to size the slide and format the background. The INSERT tab is used to insert the picture and graphical text. Both are positioned on the slide.

42 —

Amazing Websites & Apps
Easy Do-It-Yourself
David K. Ewen, M.Ed.

— 42

The slide can then be saved as a picture by clicking

— FILE
— SAVE AS
— CLICK "save type as" JPEG

Save the PowerPoint as a JPEG

43 —

Amazing Websites & Apps
Easy Do-It-Yourself
David K. Ewen, M.Ed.

— **43**

The PowerPoint **JPEG file** can then be resized, cropped, and edited using online image editors. Some good ones are:

http://**LunaPic.com** & http://**Blibs.com**
 (http://www166.LunaPic.com/editor)

https://**pixlr.com**

http://www.PicMonkey.com

44 —

Amazing Websites & Apps
Easy Do-It-Yourself
David K. Ewen, M.Ed.

— 44

Videos

45 —

Amazing Websites & Apps
Easy Do-It-Yourself
David K. Ewen, M.Ed.

— **45**

Videos from YouTube can be used on your website even if you don't own them. They way you'll use them is by linking or embedding them to your website. You cannot download and then upload to another resource to be used. They must be used in their original form on YouTube.

46 —

Amazing Websites & Apps
Easy Do-It-Yourself
David K. Ewen, M.Ed.

— **46**

There are two ways to access YouTube Videos. One is by the direct link which is like a normal web link. The other way is by using "embed" code to add to your website so that the square image of the video with a play button shows. It is like a picture that runs a video when the 'play' button is clicked.

47 —

Amazing Websites & Apps
Easy Do-It-Yourself
David K. Ewen, M.Ed.

— **47**

Under the YouTube video, there are tabs to click for sharing. One is the link and the other is indicated as "embed". The embed code is copied and later added to the right spot in the website.   It is similar to this:

<iframe width="420" height="315"
src="https://www.youtube.com/embed/v2QmQ1pv8dc" frameborder="0"
allowfullscreen></iframe>

48 —

Amazing Websites & Apps
Easy Do-It-Yourself
David K. Ewen, M.Ed.

— **48**

Code that looks like this embed code which is HTML coding that is inserted in the website editor that allows custom HTML code to be added.   There are buttons on the editor that looks like

</> or <HTML> or </HTML>

Web Development

Amazing Websites & Apps
50 —   Easy Do-It-Yourself   — 50
David K. Ewen, M.Ed.

When creating the website, a tab labelled as NEWS can be linked directly to the Facebook page. It has the latest news, images, videos, and events. Another tab can be labelled as BLOG that is linked directly to the Twitter Feed. Twitter has been defined as a micro-blogging site. Other tabs can link directly to other social media sights such as LinkedIn, Google Plus, and more. A calendar of events can be maintained and linked directly to a calendar on Google Calendar.

Authors of books may have an Author Page on Amazon.com. A tab can link directly to their Author Page. People who have classes online, such as Udemy.com, can have a tab linked directly to their profile that lists all of their classes.

The websites of today, use tabs that link to other platforms where people have a profile that shares streaming information or a catalog of data. As these platforms change and evolve, the website does not need to change. A website may only need to have a front end with tabs that link to other platforms.

The basic tools that create websites in an intuitive manner are

- www.Wix.com (also creates mobile apps
- www.Webs.com
- www.Web.com (web & Webs are 2 different platforms)
- www.Weebly.com
- www.WordPress.com
- https://www.yola.com/

Google has their own web page developer that is easy to use:
https://sites.google.com

If you are planning to receive payments online, there are PayPal interfaces. An account with PayPal.com is required.   The merchant services for PayPal has merchant services. See **https://www.paypal.com/webapps/mpp/merchant**

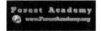

Amazing Websites & Apps
Easy Do-It-Yourself
David K. Ewen, M.Ed.

The fastest website development is template driven and uses an intuitive graphical user interface to add elements and pages to a website.   A first start to the web page development is to set up the following:

- **Facebook Page**
- **Twitter Feed**
- **LinkedIn Profile**
- **Blog (Try Blogger.com)**
- **Google Calendar**

The nice thing about a Facebook Page and Twitter Feed is that they can be easily updated and kept fresh with the simple use of a mobile device. This can be done anywhere and anytime.   By taking advantage of Facebook and Twitter along with your mobile device, you can be assured of having the most current information on you website.

53 —

Amazing Websites & Apps
Easy Do-It-Yourself
David K. Ewen, M.Ed.

— 53

App Development

Begin after webpage complete
App uses webpage content

Just like the website development we talked about, mobile apps can be made in the same way. The apps being developed are Web-Apps that are pinned to the home screen of a mobile device.   It is recommended to create the webpage first prior to developing the mobile app. The Web-App will make use of the webpage.

The web development tool WIX (**www.Wix.com**) creates both websites and mobile apps. When the website is being coded, the mobile app is being made at the same time.

COMO is a good web-app development tool. (**www.Como.com**) It has a unique auto-discovery technology that grabs existing online content to builds an app in seconds.   The online content can be from blogs and social media. There are a variety of styles, backgrounds, and color themes available.   COMO offers ROI-generating features, such as coupons, loyalty cards, e-commerce, and more. COMO offers the ability to submit an app to leading marketplaces: the Apple App Store and Google Play.

There are a large number of simple mobile app development tools that do not require downloads or complicated coding. Some have fees and many do not. Here is a partial list. Choose the one that fits your needs and that you feel comfortable using. You can search online to find others.

- http://www.appsbar.com
- http://www.appypie.com
- http://www.appsgeyser.com (Android only)
- http://www.mobincube.com
- http://www.infinitemonkeys.mobi
- https://www.yapp.us

56 —

Amazing Websites & Apps
Easy Do-It-Yourself
David K. Ewen, M.Ed.

— 56

Pin To Home Screen

57 —

Amazing Websites & Apps
Easy Do-It-Yourself
David K. Ewen, M.Ed.

— **57**

The mobile apps that are created in this course are called Web-Apps. A web app is a URL that is pinned to the home screen of the mobile device. A URL is called Universal Resource Locater. It is a fancy name for a longer website link that is not a domain name. Some examples are:

(name you pick).webs.com   or   __(your ID)_.wix.com/_(name you pick_)

The Web-App is accessible on any mobile device no matter what the operating system is.   For example, a Web-App that operates on an iPhone will also work on an Android tablet.

The process of pinning a Web-App on the home screen of a mobile device is identical to creating a shortcut of a website on the home screen of he mobile device.

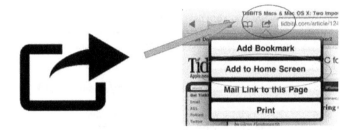

- Enter the URL in the browser.
- Click the SHARE icon
- Select Add to Home Screen
- The URL will be pinned to the Home Screen

- Enter the URL in the CHROME browser.
- Click the OPTIONS button (see 2 kinds)
- Select **Add to Home Screen**
- The URL will be pinned to the Home Screen

Amazing Websites & Apps
Easy Do-It-Yourself
David K. Ewen, M.Ed.

One of the most common and best examples of a web URL is pinning a blog to the Home Screen of a mobile device.

Google has a blogging platform called BLOGGER. A google ID is used to create blogs at **www.Blogger.com**.   The URLs that result from Blogger are in the form of:

http://__(A_Name)_.BlogSpot.com

This blogs from Blogger created by Google are mobile compliant. That means when they are pinned to the home screen of a mobile device, they are easy to read.

The difference between a blog and website is that a website has tabs. Some common tabs are   HOME | ABOUT | NEWS | CONTACT

A blog is a sequential form of posts in the form of articles.   A blog that is pinned to the home screen of a mobile device is the most simplest form of a Web-App. This course will include more complex Web-Apps.

Amazing Websites & Apps
Easy Do-It-Yourself
David K. Ewen, M.Ed.

Physical Distribution

The physical distribution of the website and mobile app is through printed material. One way is a business card and the other is by postcards. Business cards can be printed with excellent quality through a common business website VistaPrint.com.

Postcards can be made using PowerPoint. Using the DESIGN tab, set the PowerPoint slide to be 6x4. That is 6 inches a cross and 4 inches tall. This is the standard slight of 6x4 photo.

The slide can then be saved as a picture by clicking

— FILE
— SAVE AS
— CLICK "save type as" JPEG

Save the PowerPoint as a JPEG. Next upload it to a private account set up on CVS.com, Walgreens.com, or Walmart.com in the PHOTO section. You can have this PowerPoint postcard printed in as fast as an hour.

A QR Code is a square code that mobile devices scan to access websites.   An example of a QR code is here:

A QR code can be generated for any website with free resources on the web.

http://www.qrstuff.com   &   **https://www.the-qrcode-generator.com**

You can find others by searching for "Free QR Code Generator"

The QR code is used as a JPG image that is added to business cards, flyers, and postcards.   The QR code generators create QR code that can be downloaded as a JPEG file. This JPEG file is used as an art image that is inserted on the PowerPoint slide that is used to make a postcard. This postcard is then printed for about a dime a piece at CVS, Walgreens, or Walmart.

64 —

Amazing Websites & Apps
Easy Do-It-Yourself
David K. Ewen, M.Ed.

— **64**

SEO

Search Engine Optimization

Amazing Websites & Apps
Easy Do-It-Yourself
David K. Ewen, M.Ed.

Search Engine Optimization (SEO) for a website is a process and functionality that makes websites findable on search engines. The most common search engines are Google, Yahoo, and Bing. There are many other search engines, but these are the most common.

The way SEO works is the website has an 'anchor' that the search engine recognizes as a search criteria. When the website is included in a search criteria, then it will be part of a search engine results page (SERP). The 'anchors' that make a website recognizable in a search criteria are called Meta Tags. The meta tags are a piece of behind-the-scenes coding inside the website. This coding is called HTML (Hypertext Markup Language).

After the Meta Tags have been applied or coded in the website, then the website is submitted to the Search Engine. This submission results in the search engine "crawling" or recognizing the meta tags that will be recognized by a search criteria.

The Meta Tags are added to a website via the native HTML editor of the online tool used to create the website.   The Meta Tags are put at the bottom of the code.

The format of the Meta Tags is:

<meta name="Description" content="Awesome Description Here">

You can enter as many meta tags needed to make the website more recognizable in a variety of search criteria's that may be used.

An example is:

<meta name="Grooming" content="Dog Grooming Services in Boston">

It is important to have the content specific as there are many websites currently online. For example there are more "Dog Grooming Services" than there are "Dog Grooming Services in Boston".

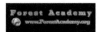

Amazing Websites & Apps
67 —   Easy Do-It-Yourself   — **67**
David K. Ewen, M.Ed.

After adding Meta Tags to a website, it is ready to be submitted to the search engines so that it can be recognized.

GOOGLE: http://www.google.com/submityourcontent/website-owner/
or more direct: https://www.google.com/webmasters/tools/submit-url?pli=1

YAHOO: http://submit.search.yahoo.com/

BING: http://www.bing.com/toolbox/submit-site-url

AOL: http://www.aoldir.com/submit/

SMO

Social Media Optimization

69 —

Amazing Websites & Apps
Easy Do-It-Yourself
David K. Ewen, M.Ed.

— **69**

SEO and SMO are different. Search Engine Optimization (SEO) for a website is a process and functionality that makes websites findable on search engines. The most common search engines are Google, Yahoo, and Bing. There are many other search engines, but these are the most common.

SMO or Social Media Optimization involves getting a website to be more visible in social media. The most common social media sites that we will talk about is Facebook and Twitter. Others are out there such as Pinerest, LinkedIn, and Google Plus. Our discussion with Facebook and Twitter can be applied to other social media sites.

The difference between Facebook and Twitter is that Facebook connects people with people and Twitter connects people with trending topics. Facebook connects people through the process of "friending", "Group Membership", and "Page Likes". The trending topics in Facebook are identified with a hashtag (#). Facebook also makes use of the hashtag.

70 —

Amazing Websites & Apps
Easy Do-It-Yourself
David K. Ewen, M.Ed.

— 70

The social media sites that take advantage of hashtags are: Twitter, Facebook, Google+, Instagram, and Vine.

The effective use of hashtags in social media sites, such as Twitter, Facebook, Google+, Instagram, and Vine, ensures reaching an unknown population of people. Hashtags connect people who share in the collaboration of trending topics. That's how they get introduced to each other. Without hashtags, people connect with others through each other. This limits their connecitivty to an audience of people that they don't know about.

Because hashtags connect people through trending topics, people meet others through a sense of relevancy. By making effective use of hashtags in social media, people will have greater opportunity to broaden their reach to others.

Amazing Websites & Apps
Easy Do-It-Yourself
David K. Ewen, M.Ed.

A good website used for finding out the best hashtags that fit best in your posted messages is **https://www.hashtags.org**

A site to search topics in hashtags is: **https://tagboard.com/**

You can search for other hashtag tools online, such as:

Hashtagify.me - show all the relevant and related hashtags to a particular keyword

RiteTag.com -- which hashtag is more likely to be seen and used by others

TweetChat.com - Tool that helps you engage with other's directly

There are so many other resources that can be found online.

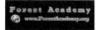

72 —

Amazing Websites & Apps
Easy Do-It-Yourself
David K. Ewen, M.Ed.

— 72

Search
Rankings

73 —

Amazing Websites & Apps
Easy Do-It-Yourself
David K. Ewen, M.Ed.

— **73**

One of the ways to increase the position of search engine rankings is to code Meta Tags in the website. This is part of the search engine optimization process. This is one of three ways to improve rankings.

The other two ways to improve search engine results rankings are:

- Pay for it (Paid advertising)
- Search Engine Recognition.

An example of paid advertising is through Google Adwords. **www.Adwords.com**

The search engine recognition is dependent on the function and operation of the search engine. For example, search for something on Bing, Yahoo, and Google. You will notice differences.

74 —

Amazing Websites & Apps
Easy Do-It-Yourself
David K. Ewen, M.Ed.

— **74**

There are two methodologies for online paid advertising. One is CPC and the other is CPA

- CPC – Cost Per Click
- CPA – Cost per Action

CPC results in payment of placement if an online visitor clicks on a link.

CPA is like CPC except there is an associated action. An example might be to fill in a survey or to download a file.

CPC and CPA is a form of pay-as-you-go advertising based on consumer response. It is different than the legacy newspaper advertising that required up front payment. This upfront payment was based on a speculation of return-on-investment (ROI) of the advertising costs. Print and broadcast advertising use this model of upfront sale of advertising. Online adverting is different because it is measurable and traceable.

Amazing Websites & Apps
Easy Do-It-Yourself
David K. Ewen, M.Ed.

The way advertising works online is through a cap on a daily budget and a bid for positioning. Ad placement is auctioned to the highest bidder. However, one who pays less may get greater online exposure.

	[A]	[B]
BUDGET or Daily CAP	$20	10
BID / Auction for position	$5	1

[A] Cap of $20 per day for $5 per hit – has a total of 4 paid spots
[B] Cap of $10 per day for $10 per hit – has a total of 10 paid spots

[B] is listed 6 more times than [A].

This means in terms of quantity of paid spots, [B] can reach a greater audience than [A] even though it paid less.   The conclusion is that no one really can predict what the best Cap and Bid to offer when placing an online ad.

76 —

Amazing Websites & Apps
Easy Do-It-Yourself
David K. Ewen, M.Ed.

— 76

Online Distribution

It takes a lot of time to submit posts to Facebook, Twitter, Google+, and LinkedIn on a regular basis to maintain a large population of posts online to be recognized. It is important to have frequent posts to show relevancy and fresh content. Most people do not do this in a manual sort of way.

How would it be if you were able to schedule posts in advance to launch on a particular date and time? Further more, how would it be if that post could automatically be populated to Facebook Wall, Facebook Page, Twitter, Google Plus, and LinkedIn. That's a total of five destinations.

It would be nice to spend one day a week to schedule in advance posts that will automatically distribute to five social media destinations. This would save a lot of time the rest of the week. It also helps increase productivity with a social media presence without spending a lot of time each day.

Now you can with HootSuite and Tweet Deck.

Amazing Websites & Apps
78 —   Easy Do-It-Yourself   — **78**
David K. Ewen, M.Ed.

HootSuite.com and **TweetDeck.com** do the exact same thing, except TweetDeck.com is specific to Twitter.

Hoot Suite has a free service that allows the posting of pre-scheduled posts that automatically distribute to five social media destinations. The most common destinations are: Facebook Wall, Facebook Page, Twitter, Google+, and LinkedIn.

The two Facebook destinations, Twitter, and Google+ use hashtags.   It is important that the posts that are scheduled out make effective use to hashtags.

With frequent posts, a website and mobile app can be readily shared with a large population of people. Using HootSuit.com and TweetDeck.com very heavily, the distribution of the website and mobile Web-App can be shared more easily and effectively.

79 —   Amazing Websites & Apps
Easy Do-It-Yourself   — 79
David K. Ewen, M.Ed.

A good website used for finding out the best hashtags that fit best in your posted messages is **https://www.hashtags.org**

A site to search topics in hashtags is: **https://tagboard.com/**

You can search for other hashtag tools online, such as:

Hashtagify.me - show all the relevant and related hashtags to a particular keyword

RiteTag.com -- which hashtag is more likely to be seen and used by others

TweetChat.com - Tool that helps you engage with other's directly

There are so many other resources that can be found online.

Amazing Websites & Apps
80 —   Easy Do-It-Yourself   — 80
David K. Ewen, M.Ed.

SDK

Software Development Kit

Professional Mobile
App Development

Amazing Websites & Apps
Easy Do-It-Yourself
David K. Ewen, M.Ed.

Professional mobile app development involve creating apps sold on app stores such as iTunes, and Google Play.   These types of apps also are downloaded and have executable files that run on the mobile device and take up storage space. These types of apps have a greater ability to perform functions beyond the Web-Apps discussed so far.

Larger app development project require Software Development Kits (SDK) to be downloaded. The apps that are developed from SDKs are operating system specific. This means an Android SDK will create Android apps only and the Apple SDK will create apps that run on iOS only.   The SDKs are also used to build apps that run on wearable technology, like smartwatches.

Here are the three common SDK environments:

- ANDROID: http://developer.android.com
- APPLE (iOS):   https://developer.apple.com
- Windows: http://dev.windows.com

82 —

Amazing Websites & Apps
Easy Do-It-Yourself
David K. Ewen, M.Ed.

— **82**

During the coding process, there may be a need to provide specialized behind the scenes coding for a fully customized experience. There are many coding languages that can be used. One of them is Python. To learn about Python, you can use some free resources including:

- http://www.codecademy.com/tracks/python
- http://learnpython.org

Other languages include Objective-C which is the iOS standard. Other languages include Java and C++. HTML5 is primarily used to create Web-Apps, but can be used in other mobile app development projects.

www.ingramcontent.com/pod-product-compliance
Lightning Source LLC
Chambersburg PA
CBHW071552080326
40690CB00056B/1810